J.P.VERBEKE

Purple Red and Blue

Children To Children

AuthorHouse™
1663 Liberty Drive
Bloomington, IN 47403
www.authorhouse.com
Phone: 1 (800) 839-8640

Published by AuthorHouse 04/22/2016

ISBN: 978-1-5049-7871-2 (sc)
ISBN: 978-1-5049-7872-9 (e)

Print information available on the last page.

This book is printed on acid-free paper.

authorHOUSE®

Note From The Author

May the full armor of God be with this story and those who hear it so that no harm or pain be caused by it in any way at anytime.

A story I have been wanting to tell you for a long time... It's time has come

Acknowledgement

I would like to thank the people in AuthorHouse in assisting me with the publication of my book. To Scott Hensley, Frannie Poulsen, Nathan Reed, and Nova Cage.

Everywhere around the world you who are orphaned know now that you are under Gods special care. Those of you who are hearing impaired, those of you who are blind, those of you who are both hearing impaired and blind, for your parents, this is the story of purple red and blue. Even though this story is for everyone, it is you who will appreciate it and understand it best. This is a story of children for children who are about to become grown ups. Welcome all. Part of this story is fiction, part of this story is true it really happened. Part of it is surreal/supernatural. I hope it will teach you of the sound silence makes at certain times, that can mean so much!

When it gets that quiet listen carefully to your deepest thoughts only then, they may not be your own. I hope it will help you know that you could find the value and the most valuable things that exist, yet are not visible.

I know this story will encourage each one of you. Simply because those who do not encourage one another are in fact, discouraging. Encouragement must be given very carefully, because it is an extremely powerful source of natural energy.

Let me tell you how I was encouraged to write this story for you. You will see with your eyes closed for yourselves who encouraged me, even though He is not visible.

Alpharetta Georgia mid October 2013

For as long as I can remember, every morning when I wake up, I first give thanks to God for this new day, then I sit at my desk and read a chapter or two of the holy Bible {it's part of the breakfast of champions.} This is what I read that morning. The part where king Solomon was selecting twelve big vases to furnish an area in Gods temple. {Jerusalem, Israel BC} The vases all had two engravings on them, these engravings were on opposite sides of one another. On one side it was a bull, on the other side was a Fleur de lice. These engravings centuries ago were meant for you today, and you will see why in a moment. I finished the chapter and went on to work.

I work for Grand Master Chung. Tae kwon do world champion. Previously I had been trained and worked for Grand Master Young Ho Jun in Tampa, Florida. My job was at the Tae Kwon Do academy at Milton Georgia. We opened at 10am and first class was at 11am. I was always the first one there, usually fifteen minutes early.

The sun was very bright that morning, not a single cloud in the sky. I pulled in the parking lot. It was so peaceful, no one was there. Our landscaping had carefully been detailed a few days ago, however it had junk all over it, cups, straws, food bags, paper on the ground. It was such a beautiful day. I wanted to do good, so I got out of my car and just at that moment, a gentle wind had blown an empty plastic trash bag to my feet. I lifted up my arms towards the sky and said thank you Lord, you knew what I was thinking and you always know what I need. I just had fifteen minutes to get this junk up, no one needed to know or see me do it. I like doing the right thing when no one is watching me. It gives me strength. Fifteen minutes later I had it all picked up, my bag was full. This is when something surreal happened. I noticed a piece of paper I had not picked up at a distance of about half a football field away. Ah! I said I can't just leave it there even though the thought had crossed my mind. So I went to go pick it up. As I got two thirds of the way to it, I could see it was the size of a business card. As I picked it up and turned it right side up it had a drawing of the Fleur de lis, this one, in addition had a pair of wings. I turned it over, there was handwritten word in French, it said, Merci! It so happens that morning I had read about the fleur de lis in my holy bible also in French. Can you see who encouraged me? I knew that God would also have me do more than pick up trash now.

In addition to teaching you how to protect your body, I should teach you how to protect your soul from God's enemies. They are everywhere and they are getting stronger. Some even have servants that do not know who they serve. Someone once said the devils biggest trick is to pretend that he does not exist and he wants you to believe that God doesn't exist either. Now some of you, just now have sadness that I must tend to. You have seen that God really exists and he is capable of even knowing your thoughts. You are wondering why then that God who loves you so much has left you, blind or deaf or in a wheel chair. Well this is complicated, it has been his concern for centuries. King Solomon did not really need carvings on the vases for a temple that has been destroyed. God used Solomon to show you how long he has loved you, and is concerned about you. This is a way he is showing you that he has not forgotten you; that he has plans and rewards for you. Your duty is to live this life completely, feeding your soul daily, so it can grow strong and healthy. You must not let anything happen to it. Your body is the home of your soul and your souls are the most valuable existing thing in the world. You will have a lot of help to protect it. Remember the code of honor required found in the Holy Bible Exodus Chapter 20. Failures at first are a natural part of a healthy learning process. Practice makes perfect.

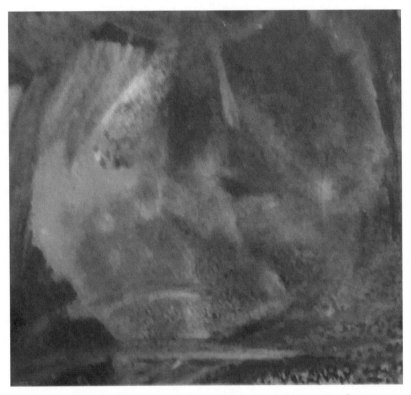

Appearance of Joe, the 16-year old boy about to become blind.

"Enlargement"

As I was leaving the post office one late afternoon, the sun was going down, people were in a rush in and out, I noticed a very tall young man. He had a blind mans cane in his right hand as his teacher was holding his left hand giving him instructions on how to use his cane. He was not blind. So I asked him why was he learning to walk with this cane. He answered me in a gentle voice: "very soon I will become completely blind." A few people heard him. They stopped and made a circle around him and his cane. Holding hands, each one began praying for him. The circle kept growing, and growing. Some people brought to this circle the little faith they had, and probably left with less. Others had more faith than most, and wanted him to have as much or more. Joe, who was almost blind, tried to cheer everyone to not be sad for him. What we could not see, Joe tried to explain to us. God was also preparing him on the inside so that when the time came he would be ready to accept what he could not change.

After everyone left, I said to Joe "no matter what happens, you must keep your faith strong and never lose it. If you let your faith weaken, you could lose it. Remind yourself of the war, that exists now, that is aimed at our soul. Your eyes could not be made to see without causing harm to it. If harm came to your sensitive soul, God who loves you so much would not be able to forgive himself. If God cannot forgive himself, who can? Who has the authority?

God does not love everyone the same way. Esau and Jacob were brothers, but did not God push back Esau and love Jacob. {Malachi chapter 1 verse two}

In all of Gods creation human beings are his favorite creation. Children are his favorite human beings. You are His very special children!

Introduction to "Purple, Red and Blue"

Purple is nineteen years old. He was born blind. Purple hads a very special gift, the gift of music. He loved music so much that he practiced it until it became a talent/skill. When he was fifteen years old, his parents had a car accident, and were taken away from him. The only family he has left is his older sister Sarah. She is just twenty-one years old. Sarah also has a gift. She has the ability to draw. Her talent is now a skill, and it's unmatched. She also likes to paint. Sarah's gift allows her to describe the appearance of everything to her brother. Most of the concepts that Purple has come from his sister's descriptions. In a way, she is his eyes. Purple always has a coach's whistle around his neck, in case he needs help with anything. Three whistle blows means come quickly. {Every child, every woman should wear one. Anyone hearing three whistle blows should respond to this call for help immediately.}

Chapter One

Swimming to the moon

Northeast part of the American continent, a cold late October morning sometime in the future at 5:55am Sarah, Sarah, Sarah ... three whistle blows. Sarah wakes up. Her bedroom is down the hall from her brothers. Wrapped up in her blanket Sarah comes running in to Purples room. What is the matter she asked. I could see, I could see, oh wow! Purple you had a dream. She laid next to him. It was fantastic! The colors Sarah were fantastic. It seemed I was swimming towards the moon. I could see. Really SEE! The water was warm, the air was cold, all kinds of colors are so beautiful. I could see them and feel them.

Up until now all that Purple had ever seen was a dull grey behind his eyes.

Purple was so excited by this new found notion. Each color had made and left an effect on him.

Colors are so fantastic. Their light is so wonderful. Some colors felt warm while others felt cold to me. I could reach some of them. Others were melting away and faded as I tried to reach them. It was magnificent! I hope to never forget this dream and its many feelings. Do you have these every night? I got an idea said Sarah, lets go downstairs to the studio. I will paint your dream in detail on a canvas, so they did. As Purple was describing the things in his dream, Sarah knew that this was the first time Purple was describing what he had actually seen to anyone. So Sarah diligently painted every detail.

Meanwhile, outside the first snow of the season had began to fall. It was very cold and very quiet. So quiet, it seemed nature was trying to say something. The sound of the air was muffled by the falling snow. All the wild animals had taken shelter. This peacefulness felt safe. A blessing had swept over the land. I was walking my dog Buddy around the perimeter, Buddy was a Rottweiler that was very gentle in demeanor and most protective of Purple. The home was built at the foothills of the Pocono mountains of Pennsylvania. The property had two smaller homes that weren't attached for the hired help, myself and others. I had been hired to keep an eye on things like a big brother. Purple's parents would be on tour most of the time. Mom was a concert Pianist, Dad was orchestra conductor. They were a world famous couple.

Living on the property, as a husband and wife team were Pat and JR. Pat was a medical assistant, devoted to Purple and Sarah's upbringing. JR. was a retired school teacher.

Finishing our perimeter walk we came in the kitchens back door so I could take off my boots and dry the dog paws. To my surprise there was Sarah at the kitchen sink, cleaning her paint brushes. She was so happy to tell me, that Purple had a dream last night, it was his first. She attempted to recreate it on a canvas. I hope I got it right. May I have a Look, I asked. I'll describe to you what I see and you can compare it to what purple told you. Lets go see she said. We were both unaware that Purple was still in the studio. He was in the back sitting in the dark. We did not notice him. Whoa! I said, this is very impressive Sarah. The paint is still drying, so I laid it flat until the paint dries, she said.

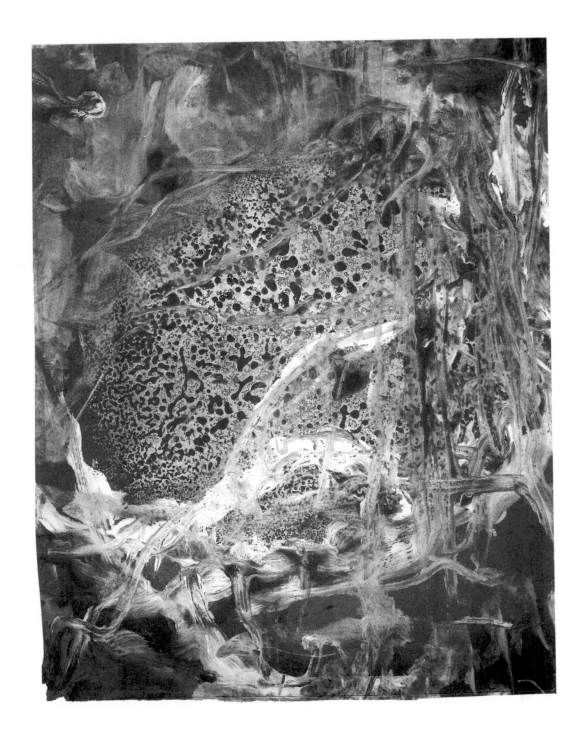

Chapter Two

A Dream within a dream.

I began to describe what I could see in this painting. Purple who was sitting in the back did not make a sound. He was fascinated by what I saw on the canvas. He had never heard anyone describe what he had seen. He had never seen anything. Sarah, I asked, how were you able to paint this evil looking angel, he seems to be carved into the ice bridge. This is where something surreal happened. This happens thru an illustration for the recreation of the painting of Purples dream. This maybe, for those of you, who have good ears, but do not quite hear what I am saying. To get the attention of those of you who have good eyes but cannot see clearly, this is not your fault. This is from the damage caused by the war on your souls.

What are you talking about, said Sarah. I did no such thing. Here I said, look wow! she said I did not paint that. He does look evil! Purple in the back said, I had forgotten all about him trapped in the ice. I never told you about him. Come to think about it there was another angel there, this one had two little horns and one of his legs was missing from his knee down. Purple, we did not know you still down here. Its perfectly alright. I was enjoying Joe's description of your painting Sarah. You have really captured my dream and placed it on a canvas. That is fascinating! I was putting music to it just listening to your details: Joe.

Sarah look, there he is coming thru now as the paint is curing, this is amazing. Half his leg is missing, and I see his two little horns. The three of us agreed. We should pray to God to help us understand the meaning of what is happening here. So we held hands and kneeled, in addition we asked that God's will be done, and that we would know what to do at the end of our prayer. We stood up. Purple knew what to do. He had been enlightened. "We're going to Paris, right away to the Louvre museum." According to the description I will receive from Sarah of certain famous paintings. I will put music to them. To help blind people see them thru my melody vision, to enrich their world and entertain them.

The big picture is this, in the Louvre Museum of Art are many of the most famous painters paintings, so we will go there. Sarah has the skills of expressing the magnificence of what she is seeing to me. On location I then will appropriate: key notes and instruments in solo, or by groups arranging them in harmony to the motionless scenery. Filtering out everything else. We will need to do this for about nine or ten paintings. We will record our notes simultaneously for each painting. When we return home from Paris we will rest, then Sarah and I will spend a few days in the music studio to translate what she has seen into sounds, I will then transform all that in to their own melodies, then to their own individual "Melody Visions" if God allow us to melodies vision will open their mental eyes, so blind people will have an opportunity to develop the skill of viewing what has not been visible to them. Originally at first God may not of approved of it, but times have changed, he may permit the viewing of beauty in a world that seems to have less of it, we are also doing this for unselfish reasons, and a good cause! Old exquisite fine art in combination with classical, instrumental, and electronic music, leads to the development of ones minds eye by inspiration.

Chapter three

Turn Your Gifts into Talents. Use Your talents for gifts.

Purple is such a talented musician that he can play almost all of the instruments that exist today. The guitar and piano, he plays them as good or better than anyone's. He can hear music once and instantly replay it. By the age of 18 he had composed, recorded and published more music than anyone before him. His music is always at the top of the charts all over the world. No one knows who Purple is. He has remained anonymous for his protection. Musicians are targeted most by God's enemies.

Each detail in a painting or scenery gives him a musical note, now with his new found notion of the emotions the feelings of each color it s affects had made on him. He was ready to do some real good music. He wanted to help first the ones of his own kind, the blue. Purple was given a divine driven purpose to illuminate, decorate, beautify, hopelify the world of the Blues everywhere. Soon he's also going to want to do everything he can for those who we called Reds.

Chapter Four

Why Do WE Do What We Do?

Deep inside Purple knows that the difference one person makes on another is either a good one or a bad one. If its not one of these two differences it will not matter. After we are gone, the differences we have made will continue on making differences until the end of time. At the end of time, which one will we have made the most of, good ones or bad ones?

How about a drop of water? When a drop of water falls from the clouds it either waters, feeds or cleans something. If it has no purpose at all it simply returns where it came from. If it does serve its purpose, it continues on its journey for awhile, before returning to its source. God does not even waste a drop of water. The description of perfection in the art world is one when one can no longer add something or subtract something.

Chapter Five

Purple goes to the rescue of Red and Blues

Joseph: Purple ordered me, contact the hanger, our pilots, and the team we are flying to Paris as soon as we can. Sarah, tell Pat and JR to pack our bags, enough for nine days. Get the Range Rover ready, for a trip to the airport and back.

We arrived at the hanger on the East coast on that day. Our pilot had finished inspections and preparations. Our jet was ready. Welcome aboard, our pilot said. We will be crossing the Atlantic ocean with a full moon tonight. At our landing in Paris, the usual fog at this time of the year is expected. We are loaded and fully fueled sir. Tower has given us the good to go signal.

Chapter Six

Flying by Moonlight and Music

"Proceed" said Purple. Purple would sit in the back where he had the state OF THE ART synthesized keyboards and surround sound system set up. Will you be playing at take off, boss? Asked the flight engineer, I would like to if it is okay with everyone. I have prepared a sample overture for take off. We approached the runway, as we paused for take off. We thank our heavenly Father for the great privilege that we were chosen for. Speeding down the runway, the sound of the wheels were the loudest. And just as the wheels left the ground, all vibrations stopped. The engines were no longer heard, overtaken by the louder sound of the synthesized keyboards. It was as if they were powering the flight. The sound Purple was making, resembled a massive waterfall at the end of a deep cave, blended with the joyful chanting of a hundred children or more singing silent night, echoing in the distance.

Sarah dimed the cabin lights. Our plane was almost vertical, accelerating to the speed of sound. The moment was breath taking. We leveled out and saw the moon rise. The light from the moon illuminated the star filled sky, reflecting back down on the ocean a golden road east. As Sarah would tell purple what she could see. He was reliving his dream, filled with inspirations. He played on for a couple of hours. We all fell asleep with very little energy left.

I was awakened by our flight engineer, asking me to take a look out the window, and witness a most beautiful sunrise.

The sun had a pink and purple halo, as it pierced a multi colored blanket of clouds . Gradually the dark part of the sky was beginning to turn light blue and the stars began fading .

I thanked God for our day I asked him for his full armor of protection, that we may not cause any harm, or be harmed by anything or anyone. I than woke up Sarah first so she could see the sun rise.

She opened her eyes and smiled at me, our captain made a sharp right turn to role Sarah to her window so she could see it with out getting out of bed. Both of us went to go wake Purple up. As soon as he came to consciousness he thanked God, we than read 2nd Peter chapter 1 verse 3-9.

We then thank God for the presence oh his holy spirit leading us to read the right verse of the right chapter for all the right reasons at the right time.

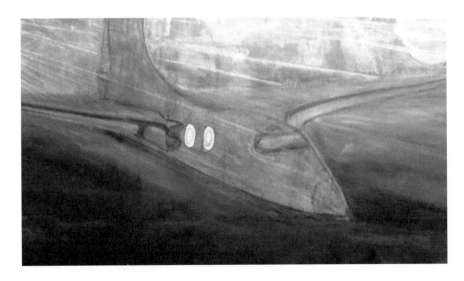

Chapter Seven

When the first Red heart comes into the picture.

In Paris, as Purple and Sarah were working, I was watching from a distance. Sarah was discreetly speaking into a microphone, recording the details of a very famous artwork. As Purple listened to the details, he was carefully recording through his microphone the musical notes that bring to life the melody visions. One day as this was going on, I noticed a young lady drawing a man's caricature. Then presenting it to him, hustling him for a few Euros. The man smiled, shook his head and said no, he walked away. She then followed him and she sprayed his close with ladies perfume without his knowledge. This man now smelled like a woman! I laughed as she tried drawing another well dressed man. Two guards came behind her, lifted her up, and carried her outside the front door and told her never to come back. I noticed her trying to sneak in the next day dressed as a tourist with sun glasses and a hat made up like a movie star. She came in unnoticed and started her hustle. Purple noticed her perfume right away. She started to draw Purple. He had captured her curiosity, and her imagination after all. What is a blind man doing in an art museum day after day? I approached her discreetly, laughing to myself about what she might make Purple look like. To my astonishment, she had recreated Purple on paper. He was drawing himself on the canvas, drawing himself on the canvas, into infinite infinity. Wow! I said to her. "How much would you like to have for that?" When she answered me, I came to the conclusion, that she was Red and could not hear me. She had told me to go fly a kite. This was not for me!

At that moment, our two unfriendly guards lifted her up again to take her out the front door, and throw her out! "Purple, Sarah we must leave now." They followed right behind me as I followed the guards who were throwing her out the front door on to the marble steps, one guard picked up her perfume bottle and pretended to handed to her, then smashed it on the water drain. This gentle Red girl instantly broke into tears. We approached her. She was crying, "That was the last bottle". She said speaking in french. "My mother's perfume. I don't think they make it any more. It is very hard to find." I translated to Sarah and Purple whom said we will get her some more. We asked her what it was called, she said. "Cristal" by Channel. "What do you want? Leave me alone". I aked her again, she looked at me then looked at Purple then she put her head down and cried unconsolably. Let us help you. Where do you live? Sarah picked up the drawing she had made before they threw her out, it was at the top of the stairs in front of the door, the door where millions of art lovers had gone through, to admire the final resting place of history's finest "Most prestigious", self promoting useless art form, that truly is extraordinarily magnificent. Sarah realized the meaning of this drawing, a blind man at the easel drawing himself into infinity. Later this penciled drawing became the most famous painting of all times! Almost every person on the planet had a copy in their home. A simple drawing done by ones admiration for another not self. It was born at the final resting place of ancient art, and had been thrown out along with the artist, to be rescued by a blind musician that wished he and others like him could try to imagine, just imagine what they could not see, to try and understand if their blindness was for their souls protection? And yes it is, there are sounds now that also are designed to weakened one's soul. We found out she was an orphan deaf girl named Adriel. She had just been let out of a convent, had just turned eighteen and her parents had died two years back. Sarah and Purple began adoption procedures, and adopted Adriel. After what they had witnessed, they had agreed to leave Paris as soon as possible.

Purple produced melody vision and gave it to the blind everywhere in the world at no charge. Others had to pay the regular price. Proceeds went to a hearing impaired schools. Inside the CD was a poster of the drawing made by Adriel it said "Our abilities have no limits". It was signed from the red heart of a red girl. She remained anonymous but she was known by everyone faster than anyone before her. Just a few hours later Blue's started raising money for Reds. Red's started to raise money for the blues. The rest of the people where in awe! They volunteered as well. It is simple really the power of the people that love one another, is far more powerful, not even comparable to the ones that hate. Thank you letters followed from everywhere. Sarah and Adriel opened a magnificent drawing school. The school had several divisions. One of these divisions was a music school, where the students that liked to draw would be challenged to compete in a drawing competition. Their drawings were inspired by the music Purple played, that he had composed by descriptions of other drawings Sarah had given to him. Drawings most resembling the original description were the winners of the competition. The same winning drawing later challenged the music students to compete in a music contest inspired by that drawing that had won the drawing contest. The best music winner was selected by a vote. The school was called Purple's Children's Red and Blue Art Academy.

Chapter 8

Sound of Music, Sound of Silence

Ten years had passed, and Adriel had fallen in love with Purple. Purple had always felt that way about Adriel. Both of them had kept these feelings a secret, hidden deep inside their hearts. Science had made so much progress, that Adriel's hearing problem could be helped now, with a surgical procedure. Immediately Purple offered Adriel this possible opportunity. Throughout the years Purple had written so much music just for her expressing his love and affection. He hoped one day he would have the greatest honor and privilege for her to listen to it with him. She did return from her successful surgery. Purple invited Adriel to his music studio. She was about to hear the sound of music for the very first time in her life. This was more than he had hoped for. As they walked to their studio, Adriel reached for and held Purple's hand. Purple put both his hands on her face and felt how beautiful she really was. He then passionately kissed her, this was the best moment of his life.

This music in which every note of every instrument where played by Purple, reflected all the love he carried in his heart and soul since the moment he had heard her cry. He had been working on it for over 10 years. She would be only one allowed to ever listen to it. Purple in prayer said "Ever lasting loving Holy Father thank you so much, this music is for you because Adriel may never hear it, if she does it will be your gift to her. May your will be done. I love you my Lord.

He stayed behind the glass as she went into the listening room. He gently turned the music on for her. In his mind eye he imagined her smiling. He slipped on his earphones and flipped on the switch Adriel continued to listen to the music. She was in awe! Tears were running down her face. What she heard was the best music ever composed and played with absolute perfection. This music was meant for God's approval.

Purple as he had turned the switch on to his headphones had blown his eardrums! He had became unconscious, now he could no longer hear or see. He was no longer a "Blue" he had become a "Red and Blue". Now he is a "Purple"! God loved Purple so much he had to protect him for a while Purple had been discovered and was in danger from God's enemies and his own ego. Adriel adored him throughout his life, their love for each other never stopped growing.

Purple had made enormous contributions to the research and development to help the hearing impaired and the blind. He would probably in a few years, be able to hear again. As you will too. He had never made anyone angry. Everyone loved him. His only enemy Is the same one we all have. He pretends he does not exist, and wants you to believe that neither does God, But God does exist, so does his love for you. When you asleep at night, you're sleeping in the palm of His right hand. It is hard to get out of bed sometimes, isn't it? When you get older you will find his love his compassion, also his sadness in the holy bible. Just pray before you read it each and every time, so that the Holy Spirit, who is the author can also be your translator you will be enlighten Thank you, May God Bless each one.

Informational and Inspirational reading in the Holy Bible: Revelation Chapter: 22 Verse 6-21 // Daniel Chapter 12 Verse 1-10 // Ephesian: Chapter: 6 verse 1-18

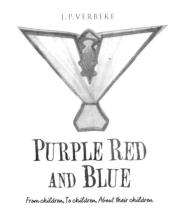

PURPLE RED AND BLUE

From children, To children, About their children

VI was a boy that was the bravest boy who ever lived. One day when he landed, children gathered around him, they asked him: why do they call you VI? I can see with my eyes closed, I have never opened my eyes. I could be tempted and loose my way if I did. How are you so brave? I have more courage than anyone. Where does your courage come from? From not having any fear of anything. How can you not have any fear? I have more faith, where did you get this faith? From my knowledge. What knowledge? My knowledge I got from searching and researching God. Did you find him? I found his love for me. It is so strong, that I love him. So much I keep looking for him. The more I look, the more of his love I find. His love is everywhere. Why do you need courage? Everywhere there is God's love to reach it you must be brave. The enemies of God attack you, to keep you from it. In hopes to destroy your love for him. This world is making it so difficult to reach God's love. They say that it is impossible, but my courage makes it possible. My braveness allows me to face God's enemies, who are my enemies as God's friends are also my friends. Search for God. He is everywhere. Develop your faith in him. Grow strong if you have fear, go work out. You need more faith. Faith gives you all the courage that you need. Remember God has many enemies.

Printed in the United States
by Baker & Taylor Publisher Services